THE DYNAMICS OF LOVE:
THE HIGH AND THE LOWS

Gwendolyn Johnson

The Dynamics of Love: The Highs and the Lows
By: Gwendolyn Johnson

Designed by: Jazzy Kitty Publishing
Logo Designs by: Andre M. Saunders/Leroy Grayson
Editor: Anelda L. Attaway

© 2016 Gwendolyn Johnson
ISBN 978-0-9970848-6-3
Library of Congress Control Number: 2016930431

All rights reserved. This book is protected under the copyright laws of the United States of America. No part of this publication may be reproduced or transmitted in any format or by any means electronic, mechanical, or otherwise, including photocopying, recording or any other storage or retrieval system without written permission of the publisher, except in the case of brief quotations embodied in critical articles or reviews. For Worldwide Distribution. Printed in the United States of America. Published by Jazzy Kitty Publishing utilizing Microsoft and Adobe Publishing Software utilizing Adobe and Microsoft Publishing Software.

ACKNOWLEDGEMENTS

I thank God for my gift of writing and that He guided me through this process.

I thank Anelda Attaway and the Jazzy Kitty Publishing staff for making my dreams of a published author to come true!

DEDICATIONS

This book is dedicated to the Lord, my children, Steven, Geneedra, Dexter, Shanequa, my grandchildren Damien, Deneedra, Elijah, Steven Jr. and some others that I don't remember, but they prayed for me and told me not to stop.

TABLE OF CONTENTS

INTRODUCTION i

CHAPTER 1 - Learning about Life, Relieving Up to 40 01
    Love as a Lost Soul 12
    To Have Everything a Person Need, but Yet Not Be Happy 16

CHAPTER 2 - My Dark Days 19
    Locked Between the Walls of My Addiction 19
    Lonely 21
    Insecurities 23
    Pain 25

CHAPTER 3 - My Deepest Thoughts 27
    Remember 27
    Sitting on Stupid 30
    Fulfillment 32
    Nonsense 32
    Changes 33
    Living Again 35
    Cloudy Thoughts 37
    Fear 39
    Control 40
    Today I Live 43
    On the Upscale 46

CHAPTER 4 - Christian Poetry - God is the Light 48
    My God Saved Me through a Dream 49
    Jesus is My Best Friend 52

TABLE OF CONTENTS

    Follow Me to Church 53

    Church of God 55

    I Go to Church 57

    Jesus is the Answer 59

    Jehovah I Ask of Thee 61

    Roses are Red, Violets are Blue 63

    Why is it that I Feel So Great! 64

    A Moment at Home 66

    In this World We Can't Make It Without God's Help 70

CHAPTER 5 - About Love and My Family 73

    My Grandmother, the Late Scotty Johnson 73

    Mom M (Mom Margaret) and Pop Pop-Mom M 74

    Pop Pop 75

    Happy Mother's Day to All the Mothers! 76

    When God Made Mothers, He Made Diamonds and Jewels 78

    Grandmother 80

CHAPTER 6 - Photos of Me and My Family 82

ABOUT THE AUTHOR 90

INTRODUCTION

My name is Miss Gwendolyn Victoria Johnson and thus far I've had an interesting life. I have been hurt, but eventually found God's love. And I realized through everything that I have been through; the heartache, betrayal and pain that God's love is real, it doesn't hurt and He loves me and you unconditionally. And because He loves us, we should love one another. But unfortunately, most people love is not genuine and normally has something attached to it. It's simply not genuine.

This book is a snippet of my life and what I had to learn about the love; people verses the love of God. And the poetry I have written in this book helped me throughout my life and my hopes are, that it will inspire you and encourage to love genuinely and find God's love. Most importantly, share His love and have it within.

CHAPTER 1/Learning about Life – Reliving Up to 40

I am Miss Gwendolyn Victoria Johnson and I always will be. I was born in Mobile, Alabama in a very Deep South area of Prichard which was primarily an all-Black community at that time in the late 1950's. However, I don' know much about that end of the world because I was just born on February 4, 1959. I was born to a young mother named Daisy Lee Johnson who was 18 years old and single. My father name was George Johnson Jr. I can't even begin to think of the look that was on my parents faces when I came into this world. As much as I would, I wish someone had taken a picture of them at that moment. However, no one did. None the less, I believe in my heart that they were very happy and that it was a beautiful day for the both of them. And maybe one of the happiest days of their lives. Because I was the first girl they had. But anyway, there I was a big bundle of joy.

But again, I had arrived so they had to give me a name. And from what I was told when I asked how I got my name, it was explained to me that my mother liked the name George so much that she gave me a name that had a "G" at the beginning. Therefore, she came up with the name Gwendolyn Victoria Johnson. And after naming me, the couple had a few days to think about if they wanted to keep that name or change it. But after all, they kept it and they began to enjoy me. They did want all new parents did, they fed me, played with me and they even changed my diapers. They also gave me the nickname which happens to be Nennie. And how they came up with that was the fact that my real name was too long for such a little person, and Nennie sure was a lot shorter than my real name. So that's how I ended up with my nickname Nennie. Okay here we go, I want to start by telling you how my father left my life. One day my father was out with the fellows and a fight broke out. So everybody started throwing bricks and other objects. They began to brake car windows out of other people's cars. Therefore, my father ended up going to jail and my mother was left to take of my older brother John and me.

My mother lived at home with her parents and trying to raise us. At that time, it was difficult to raise a family in the Deep South of Mobile Alabama and things started to get hard for her to do it alone. But with the help of the good Lord, her parents, and some of her siblings, she did a good job with us. However later, she ended up having more and more children.

So one day she met another young man, they began to talk and things got serious. And by the time my father was released from jail my mother had pushed to the side and not long after, she and the other young man got married. My mother was now marriage to someone else, so that meant that I was no longer with my mother and father. I was now with my mother and her new husband' which made her husband my stepfather. And my real father kind of vanished out of my life. He didn't care enough to stick around to even support or care for me. So that was the end of him for a while.

By the time I was three or four years old they had my brother and then my sister. Then my other 3 brothers. And I saw little of my mother. By the time they were finished having children they had 10 of us. And I was the second child of ten, and the oldest girl of 7 boys and 3 girls. And there were more siblings than me, and I had to grow up at a very early age. I grew up in Mobile, Alabama and mother did what she thought was right.

She took us to church every chance she got.

My stepfather started spending more time away from home. Therefore my siblings and I started going over to my grandparents' house all the time. And they became very concerned and they got angry and began to tell my mother if she didn't take better care of us that they would take us from her. They told her that needed to stop having babies if she couldn't feed or clothed them. In fact, they said a lot of nasty things to her. They even told her that they were going to call the State on her if she didn't straighten up. That went on for years. On day they threatened my mother about taking my brothers and sisters, until one day my grandmother took my oldest brother and myself and my sister next to me and she left with us. She took us home with her for weeks. So my mother got angry and told my grandmother to keep us and she did just that for little a while.

One day my stepfather came home and asked for the children. My mom replied that we were at her mother's and father's house. My stepfather got angry, he went and got us and they had a big argument. They said a lot of hurtful things to each other. Then my grandparents began to say, "What's in it for you?" That was directed at my stepdad. They asked my brothers and me if my stepfather had been hitting on us? They asked us many different questions like, has your mother fed you? Has that man put his hands in your panties? (Referring to my stepdad) They would say to me and my sister. "Don't you lie to me; he's been putting his hands in your clothes? Tell me the truth or I will whip you."

My uncles begin to spend the weekend with us, they were watching us on the sly, and my mother didn't know at first. Then it became a regular thing every weekend. Sometimes they were at the house every day. When they got out of school they said my grandparents sent them over there to keep an eye on us and my stepdad. My uncles told my brothers the truth about all of this as they got older.

My uncle started fighting with my stepdad, they would pick fights with him, they kept all kinds of foolishness going on all the time. One day my mother said, "I have had enough of a family getting in my business, I can't take it anymore. I've got to go." So her and my stepdad talked it over and they make plans. My mother planned to save some money and that is what she and my stepdad did. I guess when they got enough money so the time came.

I came home from my grandparents' house, me and my brothers and sisters and my mother said, "Get something to eat, get a bath." So we did and we ended up going to sleep as children do once their bellies are full and they get a bath.

So mother woke us up and said, "Get in the car." She had every sold everything she could sell and everything else was being put in the car. They packed clothes and books and many other things. Mother had sold the furniture out of the house. She had sold the beds, all except the one we had slept on. But she had told somebody they could have it or something. But anyway, mother and my stepdad loaded up all of the children last. By the time we all got in the car, we were like shook up soda which is very full, not much room at all.

By the time they left Alabama they had 9 children on the road with nine children in a little ugly red and white station wagon with bubble gum trying to hold the gas leak they had at the bottom of the car.

I was told that my grandparents were very heartbroken for long time.

They didn't speak to my mother and stepdad for years.

My mother and stepdad came to a decision to pack up and one day and left Alabama. And all of us took a very long trip to Delaware. The trip from Mobile Alabama to Delaware took 21 hours or more because of the gas leak in the bottom of the car. It made it very hard to keep gas in the car. Then Ms. C. had to keep stopping so we children could get out and go to the bathroom and they had to feed us. That had to be a very tiresome trip riding with 11 people in a car so far. From the ages of early 30's to a newborn baby. After so many hours of riding we finally arrived in Delaware.

It was very cold that day when we got to our destination. But here we all were in a very small community called Lincoln, but the area was called Greentop. Where there were so many Black people until I thought we were lost. In the State of Alabama, I did see some White people, but here I didn't see White for days.

It was the beginning of a brand new day, in October of 1969; how well do I remember getting out of the car. My parents said, "Go in the house." And we did just that. But when we got inside the house it was very small. When my brothers and sisters got inside my mom fixed everybody something to eat, we got bathed, and got ready for bed. That night my little brothers started to cry they said, "I want to go home." My mom replied, "You are home." They began to say, "No I'm not." They wouldn't go to sleep until mom laid down.

The next day we got up to go to the bathroom and we had to use a thing called a Slop Jar. I almost had a fit, I had never seen anything like that before. I peed on myself, I didn't want to use that Slop Jar. But eventually, I got over the fear of it and it was okay.

But when we wanted some water we had to go outside. Oh man, that was a trip, it was worse than using the Slop Jar. We had to pump and pump until the water came out. Then put a bucket under the spickit to catch the water, we had to do the same thing to get drinking water.

When we went around other people they laughed at us because we had a very deep accent. We were teased for a long time by our cousins, the neighbors and other people that heard us talk.

About two weeks later, we were taken to school to be together because we were new here. The children laughed at my little brothers and sisters when they went to school. We got into a lot of fights because we were always being teased about the way they talked and was told to fight for each other or we would get our butts whipped. With 8 little ones under me, I had to help fight or get into a fight for a long time. At least until some of the other siblings was old enough to take up for themselves.

As some time went by, things got a little better with the talking but the housing thing was still one of the worst thing that could ever happened in a long time.

Also, we had to go outside and learn how to chop wood to make a fire in the wood stove. I had never seen anything like that in my entire life.

The first time I saw snow. It was so beautiful and white, but it was also very cold. Then I realized why we had to wear the big heavy coats, the hats and gloves and sometimes the rubber boots, it was so we could keep me warm.

I was very glad to see the summer come. But then I had to put up with the outside toilet which was like some big ugly monster. I had never seen anything so ugly and never smelled anything so stinky. Then on top of that, my brother John was made to take the slop jar out and dump it. I cried a lot of times you because I knew once I turned the age of 10 my dad would make me dump the Slop Jar, and sure enough he did.

Then there were the wringer type washing machines and then we had to really learn how to work that water pump. We had to pump water if we wanted Lemonade in the summer time when it was hot. As much as we hated living like that I couldn't do anything about that at the time.

As the years when by continually I got older and I started to see things for myself. I saw many things with our living arrangements. Such as the sleeping arrangements in our home. Sometimes my brothers slept 4 to 5 per bed and my sister and I slept 3 to a bed.

Once we were here as a family and my stepdad got use to different people he began to change. Therefore, things at home started to change. My step dad began to drink alcohol very heavy and he gambled up all my mother's money. A lot of times we didn't have food to eat and we slept in the cold. Also we didn't have nice clothes to wear and at times we were teased by the other children. And that made us very angry little children.

One day, we all being the new children on the block we found out that many people saw my dad when he was sneaking around with different women and they would talk about it in their homes. Even their children would hear those things being said. Then their children would laugh about it. And they would tell us what they had heard their parents saying about my dad. And my brothers would get into fights all the time. But as time passed, we got use to it and things went a little better for us.

One day my friend from church went and asked my mother if I could go home with her on weekends. My mother replied, "Yes." "Therefore I started going to her house every weekend so my dad got mad and he told me I couldn't go anymore.

So at the early age of 11 I was told to babysit my little brothers and sisters. I had to wash the dishes and I had to help wash clothes. Instead of being a child I was forced to become a little Mother. In the summer time I had to go to the bean field so I would have money for school clothes. But a lot of times the money I made went towards food or the bills. When I would ask for money my dad would say, "You live here just like I do. You got to pay bills too." Also, he would take my money and my brother's money and say, "You owe me for taking care of you." As time went by we got older and my sisters were told they had to get a job. So we started out helping some of the older woman that lived in the neighborhood by helping them hang clothes on the lines, babysitting on the weekends, braiding their and children hair. And sometimes even I helped them cook. But after all of that, when I went home my dad will would beat me and at the same time he was beating me he would be saying, "You go help the other people, but you can't help at home." So I kindly stopped helping the other people for a little while.

I am now 41 years old and still reside in Delaware. Growing up I had good days and bad days, starting with school. I went to Benjamin Banneker Elementary School, middle school and then Milford Senior High School. I left Delaware in 1979 and moved back to Mobile, Alabama. I lived there from July 1977 to March 1980. And the year I left Alabama I came back pregnant.

In 1980 September 16th, I gave birth to beautiful baby boy which I named Steven Randall Johnson and all at once, I became a mother and a single parent. Which I hadn't planned but there we were, Steve and I. And I raised Steve with a year of Clearance's help but mainly with the help of God. Some of the best days we had.

In 1983, I began to care for Clarence. And one day as time passed we conceived a baby and after a 9-month long pregnancy I gave birth to a baby girl. Unfortunately, as time passed, I ended up raising our baby by myself as I had done with Steve. So now, I have a little boy and a little girl. Okay here I am with two children and no daddy for these children. But after all I had two choices, either raise these children or give them up. But being the person I am I stuck it out and I took care of my two babies, I made the best of it. I went to work from 11 p.m. to 7 a.m. Then went home in the morning to get my children went home and took care of them until I went to sleep.

After two years in 1985 I met another man; he talked so nice, he gave me love that my daddy never gave me. I thought this is okay. A month later, he beat me. He started slapping me for breakfast and supper. He almost killed me in front of both of my children. I had him arrested. So I lived by myself again.

Later then I met another man which tried to talk to me and everybody else that looked like a woman. So one night he came in my house and he told me these words he said, "I love you." And I said, "You don't know what love is." So he put his hand in my face and I told him to be there when I get back and he was. I found my gun and I shot at him. He was very close to getting hit by the bullet.

The year is now 1986 and by this time I had gotten over the feeling of being hurt by Mr. Bee. I fell for Mr. P., we dated for almost a year before we got interment. And as soon as we did, I came up expecting again. Here comes child number three, my new little bundle, a baby boy. Okay, now I have Dexter, a big 7lb 6oz baby boy. So now I am very hurt and mad at everyone in the world. Especially the men that helped me conceive my children. However, one day I came to my senses and realized that my children had to be taken care of. So I got up off my do nothing and I did something. I made a 100% turn. I went to work again at Alan Family Foods. I worked and took care of my family until a tragedy happened. I lost a very close relative then 6 days later I lost a brother, both to death. As a result, I had a nervous breakdown. I lost my job shortly after that. So there I was home with my children again with no job on Welfare. Crying nights wondering how and why I was left with my children alone. Someone so pretty, so precious and so loving. How could men be so cold hearted and so cruel to someone so innocent. Poor little baby that never hurt anyone; babies that never even asked to be born. I grew a very bitter feeling inside. I began to hate people, so bad until I wanted to kill every man in the world. Because I thought every man in this world was cold, cruel and didn't love people. Like the men that I had gotten involved with. After a short time, I began hating my boys, my brothers and uncles. Men had become a bad name to me.

    By the year of 1989 I was really fed up with these people called men. They had turned me into a real monster. So a nice guy spoke to me one day and I went off in the middle of the road. I cursed him I called him everything I could call him. And he told me I was cute while I was mad. And I told him don't be stupid nobody is cute but a monkey. And I left and went home and thought about what he said so I gave life another look, but the next time I was A little bit more careful at getting (don't know this word) with anyone that was a man.

It is now 1990, and one day I felt like I had taken all I could take. So I thought what's next? I have tried everything and nothing worked. Which way do I go now? And a voice spoke to me and said go to God. I did and those were the best days of my life when I turned to God. I felt like a brand new person I had never felt so good in my life. And for 6 years straight I lived a beautiful life. My children were happy children, I was happy and I loved life. It had become the best thing that ever happened to me. Once again I could feel love. I could see love and life had a good outlook on it. My children and I went to church on a regular basis. We gave God all the credit for everything He did for us. So we give God the praise and things went very smooth for us for the first time.

Therefore, I had learned that God loves us, therefore we are supposed to love one another. But I found as people love you, it has to be for a reason. And you have to give them, love them or trust them. However, God doesn't ask us to give what He doesn't give, but people will ask you to give what they want given and more.

This book is filled with poetry that helped me throughout my life. May it inspire you the way it has inspired me.

LOVE AS A LOST SOUL

I was born in Mobile, Alabama
In a very Deep Area of the South.

At the time,
Which was in the late 1950's and 1960's,
The community was an all-Black community.
I don't know much about that
Because I was just a Baby.

I was born to a Young Teenager
Who was a Single Mother;
Her name is Ms. Daisy L. Johnson.
My father's name is Mr. George Johnson.

I can't even Begin to think of the Look
That was on my Parents Faces
When I came into the World.

As much as I Wish that Somebody
Would have taken a Picture of them at that Moment.
But No One did that.

However,
I Believe in my Heart that
They were very Happy,
And that was a Beautiful Day
For the both of them.

And maybe one of the most
Happiest days of their Lives
Because I was the first Girl they had.

But anyway,
There I was 'a Big Bundle of Joy'.
But again, I had arrived
So they had to give me a Name.

And from what I was Told
When I asked how I got my Name,
My mother liked the name George
So much that she gave me a Name
That had a 'G' at the Beginning.

Therefore, she came up with the Name
Gwendolyn Victoria Johnson.

After Naming me,
The couple had a Few days to Think
If they wanted to Keep it or Change it.

However, only after a Few hours
They made a Decision to
Let me Keep that Name.

And a Few days later,
I was theirs to Keep.
And then they began to Enjoy me;

They Fed, Played with me,
And they even had to Change Diapers.

Later,
They gave me a Nickname
Which happens to be Nennie.

And how they came up with that
Was the fact that my Real Name
Was too long for such a little Person,
And Nennie sure was a lot Shorter
Than my Real Name.

So that's how I ended up with
My Nickname Nennie.

To Have Everything a Person Need, But Yet Not Be Happy

I am one of the most lovable people you could ever meet. I smile through a many of tears, have a very sweet personality, love the cruelest person, but never get that love back from others. How much love I give, no one seems to know how to love me the way I love them.

I have a son whom I love so dear. I gave my heart, my education and everything I ever hoped for up to love this child. Because he was so dear to me and because I love him so much. And believe it or not, my son grew up caused me many heartaches and pain. He grew up and loved people more than he loved me. So much until he would work when he shouldn't have. And the thanks I got was my son took care of other people with his hard earned money. And me, his mother and younger sisters and brothers went without. While the other people used and mistreated him; it got so bad one time until my son came home crying and once his money was gone, where was his friends? Those supposed to be friends used my son for thousands of dollars. But still I was there for my dear son who left me for everybody else. I helped him get back up on his feet and he did the same thing all over again. And guess who was there again? Sweet mom.

But I am tired of my son and everybody else that say love me. I am coming to halt with my love and kindness. My heart can't take it anymore.

I got married to an older man thinking he would be the dream come true. Little did I know that I wish many of days I never knew he lived on the same earth with me. He hurt me more in 2 years than any man has ever hurt me in 45 years. Because he cheated on me with many others. Black, White, old, young, nasty crack heads, drunks, and even my own sister. It didn't stop there, he disrespected me by trying to touch my son's girl and my daughter. He played with himself in front of whoever, family members and anybody else that would come near him. It got so bad I love him over and over and over. I found myself back with him again even when I didn't want to be. A lot of times was because I didn't (add word), I wouldn't have food to eat and he would feed me. But I paid the price for the food, he would have sex with me all night even when I was sleep. Even if I said no, he will wait until I would go to sleep and began sexing me. Whatever way that pleased him. No matter what I felt, he would go front, back, whichever was there. Me saying no didn't make much difference. That's why I feel like no love sometimes is better than fake love. If you are not going to give the real thing you should give nothing. Real love from my understanding isn't supposed to hurt to the point where it makes you hate the same person or people you love so. But sometimes I feel just like that.

I have been drained, not only has my husband used and misused me when it came to sex. But he still uses me to a point where he takes me out for a night or two, he will buy me dinner and pay for room and sex me almost all night. We will go to the store and he will give me 20 dollars, sometimes even 50 dollars, then ask me, "Aren't you going to buy something?" When I do, he will also buy himself something then I end up paying for most of the time. Therefore, he was giving me nothing. He and I will go to the store and he was by himself whatever his heart desire. I get maybe $20 out of the deal or less, sometimes even nothing. A lot of times I get embarrassed if I confront him, so to keep peace I say nothing.

He will talk to other women when we are together. He never tells the women that we are together or that he is married. But soon as he talks to a man, the first thing he will do is introduce me to the man and make sure the man knows I'm his wife. With the woman it's always said this is Gwen. Gwen this is Mary. And that hurts people in general and I think the world of this man. Even some of them that knows what he's capable of, they act as if he has never done anything. They just push the dirt under the rug and put it back down.

He cosigned for me to get a $33,000 car and told me he would help pay for it because he makes more money that I do. And it has been 3½ years and he hasn't helped me make one payment. He lied and told me don't mess up his credit. And before I let the car go give it to him. But that's just the first part, the second part is better. Jay told me not one time that he would help me with the car payments but he told me 3 maybe even 4 times that he would help me, but he hasn't helped yet. So in trying to pay for the car, I get paid, cash my check, buy a money order and send it off to the finance place. Then I have to wait for two more weeks to get another check. In the meantime, I wait very patiently for whatever he gives me to eat or give anything. I can't wash my clothes sometimes for almost 3 weeks. You think he would help? No! If I don't ask he won't give. Is that what you call love? Should a woman or man live like that and be okay?

CHAPTER 2/My Dark Days

LOCKED BETWEEN THE WALLS OF MY ADDICTION

Lost and Forgotten while the Forces hold me Still.

A Prisoner of time Trapped against my Will.

Fighting each day just to Survive and make it Through.

Exercising all the things I learnt as I Grew.

No boundaries had Limits,

For a mind so Achieved.

First the Lying and Stealing,

We became little Thieves.

Then the Running and Hiding,

Getting away from our Fears

Then the Shame and the Guilt

And evidentially, the Tears.

We battled to Survive,

But the fight NEVER ENDS,

Just Hurt and Violence and Death.

So who WINS?

There was Death on each Corner,

A new Birth on my Block.
To my friends and acquaintances,
He was known as 'Rock'.

He's the Baddest of all and most Wanted.
You see, he's the most Thought of
And replaces Everything for me.

More Dangerous than Explosives,
More deadly than Quinine.
Took EVERYTHING from me
And now he wants my Mind.

My life was a living hell
And I'm almost Insane.
And I give all praise to 'Rock'
YES, Cocaine.

This is my Story,
All Real and Non-fiction, Entitled,
"Locked between the Walls of My Addiction."

LONELY

What can I do Today
To keep me Feeling Right.
To keep my Mind in Check
And take me through Tonight.

For there are A Lot of things,
Out there that I can Do.
I'm Tired of the Same Old Thing,
I want Something New.

I could Sit here
And Bore myself to Death.
I did that Yesterday
And Too Much time was Left.

I want to do Something
And that I Surely know
To Keep me from being Depressed,
I am Tired of Feeling Low.

What can I do Today?

I haven't a Thought in Mind.
Everyone is doing Something,
I FEEL SO LEFT BEHIND.

I Sit here and Ponder Thoughts,
I do it Every day.
But while I'm Wasting Time,
Everyone's on their Way.

So I Better Make up my Mind,
Time won't Sit Still.
I still have All Day
AND LOTS OF TIME TO KILL.

Still Stretching and Yawning,
So much Energy It Takes.
I'll have Lots to Do,
JUST AS SOON AS I AWAKEN

INSECURITIES

Will life end Tomorrow
Or the Next Day?
Am I a part of Life
Or Just in the Way?

Will I get Better
Or always be Ill?
Should I Continue on
Write myself a Will?

Is there Reasons for Feeling
Good than Bad?
Or why I get Excited
And the next Second Sad?

Or Why I Worry,
Knowing it does me NO Good.
And I say I want to Change
And I wish I Could.

There's Times when I Sat

With a Tear in my Eye.
And I'm all torn Inside,
But yet I can't Cry.

Times when my Emotions Fold
And I am Falling Apart.
Yet I still can't Cry, WHY?
That's the way I was Taught

I wanted to tell Someone,
But I was Scared to Say,
"Hey Buddy can you help me;"
So I sat Dismayed.

Then I go away Holding
These things Inside,
I had a Chance to Talk,
My coverage Died.

PAIN

Why must I Suffer for the things
I thought so Right?
When my first Impulse was
To Shut Down Stuff and Fight.

The Feelings seem to Cut,
Running Straight to my Heart.
I'd Grit my Teeth and Bite down,
Lash out, then I Fought.

These Inner Pressures were too Much,
I thought I couldn't Bare.
My chest Expanded So Much,
I thought that it would to Tear.

So these Hurting Feelings
That Haunted Me Night and Day
Where all the Wrongs I've done,
To People along the Way.

And yet I still Regret these things,
I get Better Every day.
A little More and More,
Each time I Kneel and Pray.

And this makes me feel Better,
But it's also for you.
But if I want to get Well,
There's a lot of Work to Do.

First I must Accept the Things
I can't Change Myself.
Those Character Deflects,
Like Hurt, Loss, Grief, and Death.

I'll turn these Over to Someone
I know He just won't Tell.
In Return, I gain Faith,
And I'm Starting to get Well.

CHAPTER 3/My Deepest Thoughts

REMEMBER

REMEMBER
When Life was Happy,
Every Day was New?
And Friends were like Flowers,
Sprouting up everywhere.

Good times were Plentiful
And Bad times were Few.
And every Person in your Life
Seemed to Care!

Moments like this,
Always seem to Bring Us Through.
They kept us Smiling
And so Full of Joy.

They were Pure,
Like the early Morning Dew.
And NO ONE Cared,
Whether you were Girl or Boy.

REMEMBER when chasing Butterflies
Brought Joy and Laughter?
And you found Fun in Games,
Like Hide and Seek.

You Vowed to be Friends,
Now, Forever, and After
And Hiding was all the Fun
And yelling, "DON'T PEEK."

REMEMBER
When we skipped Pebbles
Across the Pond,
We all knew?

And we Built forts of Boards
And Sticks that were Dree.

We got more Candy for a Nickel then Two
And we Talked about Witches, Ghosts,
And Monsters of the Sea.
REMEMBER

When life was Pleasant
And NO Mystery?

And we NEVER wanted
To go to Sleep at Night.
The WHOLE World was Mine
To Conquer and See.

And kids played Together
With NO Reasons to Fight.

REMEMBER
The things that Brought
Smiles to your Face
And the Cheers of Happiness
That Rang in the Air?

The PLAYGROUND at School
Was the Meeting Place.
We enjoyed that Hour of Fun
And thought it was Fair.
REMEMBER?

SITTING ON STUPID

Where are you Going?

I've heard SO MANY Times.

I hid my problems, thoughts

And showed NO SIGNS.

"Oh I'm okay," was what I usually said.

I wanted to go Home

And Crawl back in Bed.

Spent all of my Money

And I'm still NOT HIGH.

But I have an Excuse

Or I'll tell you a Lie.

I NEVER Meant to get Broke

Or stay out SO LATE,

Telling you I am NOT Hungry,

But haven't Ate.

This is the Lie I told myself

For so very Long.

I found out I'm NOT WEAK,

But Virtually STRONG.

If I could STOP
And get my Head on Straight,
I could lose a Feeling
IT'S TOO LATE.

BUT I'M FINE,
So try to Prove me WRONG.
I guess I like Singing
The Same Old Song.

And do I STOP Knowing
What I will Get.
Well I'm going Home AGAIN
HAVE FUN YOU BET.

FULFILLMENT

I wasn't BORN Yesterday,
But I could DIE Tomorrow.

So if I LIVE Today,
As if there was NO Tomorrow;
I'd live my DAY to the Fullest
And do what I have to do Today.

NONSENSE

Today I want to Write a Piece.
But it came to my Surprise,
The WORDS, my MIND
Just WON'T Release
And I felt Minimized.

I've tried to WRTE in Every Way,
But the WORDS just WON'T COME.
Do I have WRITER'S BLOCK today?
TWIDDLEY DEE TWIDDLEY DEE DUM.

CHANGES

Today I Found Out,
I was someone I FORGOT.
So long I Thought I was Me,
Today I know I'M NOT.

I've ran Away from me,
Vowing NEVER TO RETURN,
But that's NO GOOD,
Cause from me I need to Learn.

Things I've Learnt before,
Were things I see you do.
They DON'T work for me,
Although they work for you.

Don't get me Wrong,
Cause I WATCHED you very Close.
And when I couldn't do Right,
This HURT me the Most.

I've found You and Me,

Now you have to Go.
How Long it will Take?
I surely don't know.

But ONE THING is Certain,
Now's the time to Start.
I need to Know WHO I AM,
From what I was Taught.

LIVING AGAIN

I see a VISION,
But it's not really Clear.
And it's NOT Today,
Cause I see that I'm Here.

It's Showing of the Future,
Where I'm Working to get it.
But I can't see Between,
I haven't Directions Yet.

Just standing Here,
The feelings SO Intense.
Wondering and Waiting,
Keeps me in Suspense.

I WON'T Give up Hope,
It's Feels like I can Touch
All the Things in Life
THAT I WANTED SO MUCH.

I guess I'll Wait and See,
What this VISION can be.
For it's NOT the First Time,
It was there for me.

But I PUSHED it away,
It seemed TOO HARD to get.
And I Dreamed of these things
AND HAVEN'T SEEN THEM YET!

CLOUDY THOUGHTS

As I Peer upon the Sky,
The Sunrays warms my Face.
I wonder what's going on,
In this Distant Place.

It looks so Soft,
These Pillows of White and Blue.
I wonder who Lives there
And what's there to Do.

Some say it's just the Sky,
But there's MORE I see.
They're Floating around
So Free and Peacefully.

It's when I Sat
And Look for things to Find.
I find Beauty and Shapes
Of every Kind.

That quietness Within
That FILLS my Heart with Joy.
Look! There goes a Boat,
"HEY, HEY SHIP AHOY."

Wow! There's an Elephant, a Tiger, and a Bear.
There's PLENTY to Explore,
Won't you PULL UP A CHAIR.

Look! There's a Snowman,
And it is Ninety Degrees.
And over there a Monkey
Or it's a Chimpanzee.

A Sailor, a Bird,
AND YOU SAY THERE'S NOTHING TO SEE.
Never Mind You,
IT'S A JUNGLE OF FUN JUST FOR ME.

FEAR

FEAR is what we Feel,
When we Don't know What We Feel.
But yet, we're Scared and Upset
And sure our Feelings are REAL.

We Cover them with Things
That make us Feel REAL GOOD,
Cause all of our Lives we were
Told that we Should.

We RUN from the Hurt and Anger
That tears up Inside.
And we find Places in our Mind,
Where there's NO PAIN to Hide.

With Thoughts and Dreams of Paradise,
We always Seek to Find.
But yet, the FEAR and Hurts of Life,
ALWAYS COME BACK IN TIME.

We run Further away,

Vowing to NEVER look Back again.

Knowing, if we let our Past CATCH US,

The Pain will SURELY Win.

The Shame and Disappointment,

NO LONGER has a Place.

For they're so FAR Behind

That LOVE is Winning the Race.

The Race Gradually Slowed Down

And I could see the FEAR Cross the Line.

So all the Running and Hiding,

Was just a Waste of Time.

Cause there Waiting at the Finish Line,

Waiting at the very End,

Was all the things I Ran from,

There Waiting for me to Begin.

CONTROL

Who is he to Judge
People Lives,
But yet,
Try to himself to be True.

You know,
It's Probably he that Strives
Basically, On the things
That People Do.

Yet everyone is Free
To do what they Want,
But if we Dislike it,
Surely them we will Taunted.

We'll say Things
Trying to make them Fall Apart.
Know Angers a Weapon
That Breaks a lot of Hearts.

And we're NOT SATISFIED
Until all is Said,
Still Mustering under Breath
Until we Crawl OFF TO Bed.

But we've Covered ourselves
With our Blanket of Pride
Knowing all is NOT WELL
And we're Hurting Inside.

Yet it's Easier to Say,
I'M SORRY OR WRONG.
Then to Comfort the Hurt
That we've Created and Carried So Long.

These uneasy Feelings
Can be set Loose and Free,
By giving up Control
And Allowing yourself to See.

TODAY I LIVE

Yesterday was FULL of Pain
And MISDIRECTED Feelings,
UNRESOLVED Problems
And all my WRONG Dealings.

Chaos and Confusion
Was how I was Living,
Always HELPING Others
And Living for CAREGIVING.

Putting my Morals aside
To help a Friend in Need
Worrying about Working
And all of them Mouths to Feed.

Trying to be Friend
And Giving all my Help
Always Looking for a Home,
For the Family that I Kept.

Dragging from Day to Day,
Doing all I Could
Promising I'd be There,
Cause I thought I Should.

Hurting when things went Wrong,
But I HELPED Anyway
Just the Same Results
At the End of the Day.

I GAVE ALL I Could,
All my HEART and SOUL
Until all my Pains in Life
Started to take its Toll.

I GAVE ALL OF ME
And Expected NOTHING in Return
So where's all these Friends
AND WHY AM I ALONE?

Where are these Friends,
I gave so FREELY to?

Why am I facing Life
AND NOT KNOWING WHAT TO DO?

Today I'm Making up my Mind,
I NO LONGER want to Give
For I've Given ALL of Me
AND TODAY I WANT TO LIVE.

Do not ask me for Help,
Or to Live your Life for you
For I have Mine
AND I'M LEARNING THINGS TO DO.

And if I Hear You Coming,
I'll act like I Don't See.
For I've Done All I Can
AND TODAY I LIVE FOR ME.

ON THE UPSCALE

A lot of Days begin,
Before I Open my Eyes.
They Start out Rushing
And Catch me by Surprise.

I grit my Teeth, Complain,
You know I want to Fight.
Usually, I find myself Smiling,
Before I Sleep at Night.

Days like This,
I find myself in trying hard to Concentrate.
I set my Alarm to get up at 5
And still get up Late.

I rush to Catch up Time
That I have Misplaced.
To get back in Balance
And set a Steady Pace.

These Troublesome Days come,
But surely they are Few.
I know that I'm Confused.
SO HOW ABOUT YOU?

But if I'm Wrong,
I Wish you would Come and Tell me,
What I Need to Know
To get on the Upscale.

So if you like going a See-Saw,
Going Up and Down
And Life has NO Motion,
Like going Round and Round.

And your Emotions
Don't seem to Feel Swell.
Then find the Elevator
That leads to the Upscale!

CHAPTER 4/Christian Poetry

GOD IS THE LIGHT

God is the Light
If Light is ABSORBED
Through a Spectrum

And one Color is taken Away,
It would Disturb
The Balance of Color.

Then so,
If any Color from
The Array of Nationalities
Were REMOVED...

Would it NOT Throw Off
The Balance of Mankind...
GOD'S CREATION?

MY GOD SAVED ME THROUGH A DREAM

I suddenly Awaken
And was so Full of Fright
And my Bed was a Mess,
I Crutched my Pillow Tight.

I was Running, Hiding
From something it Seemed.
When a Tiny Voice call out,
"I'm Here," in my Dream.

I was Startled up First,
I knew know what to Think
I Stared at the Door
Too Scared to even Blink

So Paralyzed with Fear,
This was so Strange to Me.
A Voice that I could Hear,
But NO ONE could I See.

Was I still Asleep?
Because it Felt So Real.
I felt so Weak
And my Room stood Still.

Still lying Confused
From this Voice I couldn't See it.
IT CAME AGAIN,
"REST EASY, YOU'RE SAFE, IT'S ONLY ME."

This Voice I Realized,
I've Heard MANY times Before.
But this time it was Faint
And I still WASN'T Sure.

I remember Hearing someone,
But then Came my Tears.
This was that Voice that came to me
In times of Fear.

These Dreams are Nightmares
That Haunt Me Now and Then.

They're all of the Bad things,
My Evils, Lies, and Sins.

One thing I Noticed is,
I never got to Scream.
That's why I come to Believe…
God SAVED Me in my DREAMS!

JESUS IS MY BEST FRIEND

Jesus is my Best Friend.

When I go to Him, He NEVER turns me Away!

He always Turns me in.

Even AFTER I had Sinned.

That's the Kind of Jesus I Serve.

My Sisters and Brother, where would we be?

If it wasn't for the Mercy

Of our Heavenly?

If the Lord Would Come for you Today...

What would you Say?

Forgive me Lord?

I went to Church on Today.

The Lord MET me There

And I could Tell just when

His Spirit left, I felt Empty

I began to Look and Say,

Where are you Lord.

FOLLOW ME TO CHURCH

Woman and Men, Boys and Girls

Get up off of that Curve

And Follow me to Church.

And feel the of Spirit of the God I Serve.

You might want to try it.

It's called the SPIRIT,

And you can also Get it.

Don't let the Devil

Make you go to Hell.

If you can get away from Him,

Jump Bail

Because the Devil is EVIL,

He will not see you do Right.

And will cause you to FIGHT, FIGHT, FIGHT,

Anything but DO RIGHT.

Sinner Man, Woman
Do you Think what you're doing is Fun?
I DON'T THINK SO!

Be Careful, because the Enemy know
You're holding a Gun!
It is just a Matter of Time
He will cause you to do a Big Crime.

Please say YES to God!
Say yes Lord I will Obey.

Don't Listen to Satan,
He will cause you to act a Fool,
And that's NOT COOL.
Don't do it, Stay in School.

CHURCH OF GOD

If our Lord came for you Today,
Would you be able to Say?
God I am Saved today and its OK.

Or would you have to Hide your
Dirt from Him
Because you know what He see
Would Hurt.

We must stay Clean and Saints of God
Though sometimes it gets Hard.
We can't Hide from Him.

God is TOO BIG of a God,
We have to Make up our Minds
To stay with God.

Or one Day He will SHOW UP
And we may be Saying...
Lord WAIT on me.

I have gone Astray.

You know me this is my Way.

Or Hopefully we will Honestly

Be able to Say...

The Devil thought He had me

But God Helped me

And I got Away

I GO TO CHURCH

I go to Church and it don't Hurt.

I go to Work and I feel Pain.

That must be the Name the Game.

I can't begin to Understand

The Way of this World.

Jesus is the Answer.

Do you have a Question?

Ask Him ANYTHING

And He Will Answer.

Are you Living in Sin?

And want a Way Out

And don't know how to Begin.

Call on Jesus, He will Deliver.

As people of God.

If Jesus would Come for you Today,

What would you Say?

Yes, Lord OK

Or Would you have to STOP

Cursing & Fighting and Say

Lord you know me!

This is my Way.

I have gone Astray

Or can you Honestly Say

The Devil THOUGHT He had me,

But I got Away.

JESUS IS THE ANSWER

Jesus is the Answer.
Do you have a Question?
Ask Him ANYTHING
And He Will Answer.

Are you Living in Sin?
And want a Way Out?
And don't know how to Begin?

Call on Jesus,
He will Deliver.

As people of God.
If Jesus would come for you Today,
What would you Say?

Would it be Yes Lord OK
Or would you have to STOP
Cursing & Fighting and Say
Lord you know me; this is my Way.

I have gone Astray

Or can you Honestly Say

The Devil THOUGHT he had Me,

But I got Away.

JEHOVAH I ASK OF THEE

Jehovah I ask of Thee
To remove the Bondages
That Hold Me Back
And in Allowance, set me Free.

The Bondage of Self
That has Cursed me so Long
My reasons for False Love
I ask You to Reveal and Show my Wrong

My Guards I set Forth
To keep Things my Way.
And to Protect me from Hurt
I use this very Day.

Allow me to be Given
For I've Taken So Long
For Its Cause Grief
And I Feel it's ALL Wrong

I've always wanted too Much

And it's been All for me.

But I can't Use It All

I ask You to Please set them Free

ROSES ARE RED, VIOLETS ARE BLUE

Roses are Red, Violets are Blue
I am going to Church, what about you?
I have done a lot of Wrong.
But that's okay, it's all Behind.
Every day I am getting Strong!

Don't look at my Imperfections,
But watch out for my Possibility.

Roses are Red; Violets are Blue
Don't look at my Mistakes
But look at the Things You Do.

I went to Church, I made a Change.
Are you ready for the Change Too?

Say YES! Give it your Best.
God will do the Rest.
With God's help, I am getting Stronger every day.
That's the Best way. GET SAVED AND STAY.

WHY IS IT THAT I FEEL SO GREAT!

Why is it that after a Hard day of Struggling
And a Restless Night of NO Sleep
And after the Frustration
From the Schedule I'm Juggling,

Do I find this Peaceful Feeling?
That's Resting from in Deep.

Why do I have to Beat
My Head against the Wall
And continue to Fight for
What I feel is Right?

When all I want to do is
NOT have to Fall
Just to Learn how to
Walk through Life.

But yet,
I Stand Here Full of Bliss
With a Tear in my Eye

And NEW Thoughts and Feelings
That weren't there Last Night.

For it was a being's Actions
That I found to be Lies
But it was You I sought Help through
And Today I feel Light.

Everything has a Reason,
That's the way it's always Been.
It started from day one,
The moment Eve Sinned.

And if I didn't Start the Process,
How can I Change the End?
My Battles aren't with you,
But together we Win.

A MOMENT AT HOME

This morning I Awoken, against my Will.
To find a Friend,
Watching over me Still.

A Friend I chose to Separate from
Hoping He'd follow,
He DID NOT come.

His Strength led me through life's Despair.
But I chose to Fight when thought of Unfair.

His Blessings surrounded me,
Infinite results.
Somewhere I got Lost,
Forgetting what I Sought.

Allowing myself to
Weaken and Fell again.
To the same Old Battles,
I NEVER did Win.

But it always Ends,
The SAME WAY you See.
With me in Frustration and Him holding me.

For I know I didn't Fall,
I was Waiting to Hit
And I've Felt this Before,
It's REAL, you Bet!

The same old Bridge,
I Stood upon Before.
Unmistakably Blind,
Falling for the same ole Cure.

But this Morning I say,
I awaken with a Friend.
Still longing for Peace,
Oh how long it's Been.

Forgetting how I Felt
when I last Fell on my Face
And the Hands that Comforted me,
Bringing me to this Place.

And this Voice always tells me
And I'm Starting to See.
Saying, "Wait in Silence, be Patient, have Faith
For I'm ALWAYS with you,
JUST BELIEVE IN ME.

These Gifts of Life,
Simply for and Wait.
I've Trusted in man's Ways,
In Hopes to find Glory.

But the Results always were
Hurt, Pain, and Destruction.
Somehow I found the same Mold,
NO CHANGE in my Story.

All from following He,
Who is of Greed, Lust and Corruption.

So this Morning I Ask
Of all my Trust in Thee
Allow me Freedom
From the Things that Bond me.

Give me the Courage
And the Strength that I Need.
To You, I give Grace
And of Bondage I'm Freed.

IN THIS WORLD WE CAN'T MAKE IT WITHOUT GOD'S HELP

In this World EVERYONE wants to Be
Like the Next Person.
IT'S NOT POSSIBLE.

When I was Growing up
As a Little Girl
Mother gave me Plats on my Head
For a long time.

One day she Realized
I was NO LONGER her Little Girl,
But I had Grown to be her Big Girl.
So now I wanted to wear Curls.

I never knew these Curls
Would make such a Difference.
But they did.

And ah a Mess
A hairdo can make.
The young men began

To Notice me very much.
Then came Trouble.

We started to Date
And My, My and My,
Something is really starting to Hate.

Happiness became Sadness, Truth became Lies,
My Destiny became an Eternity hell.
How important Mission of being
A Mother, Wife, an Evangelist
And an Emotional Speaker.

All fell I became a NOBODY
In my Mind, a Loser,
And worse of all of an Unwed Mother
Of Three plus one Child

But one Day,
Jesus Christ came through for me,
And beyond all of my Sin
And God's Forgiveness

I was Separated from Sin
And then my Heavenly Walk
With God began.

I thank God for His Precious Son
And His Death on the Cross
God don't Fail, I do.
That's a person that will do
To You, You, and You.
Be careful,
We can't make it WITHOUT His help.

CHAPTER 5 About Love and Family

(My Grandmother, the Late Scottie Johnson)

I remember my grandmother used to go to the house of White people back in the early 60's. She used to go there and clean those people houses for them. My grandmother Scottie Johnson was a very good woman. She was a very honest in doing what she did for the White people when she was in their house at all times. And she always told me to never touch anything in the house when I was there with her. At that time, I didn't understand, but now I do understand and it is a hard pill to swallow. Because I know that it was a very unfair how we as Black's were treated. But the thing that hurts the most is my mother did some of the same work her mother did. That was like a slap in the face because my mother also went to some White people houses. And she also cleaned their houses, cooked for them, and took care of their children. In addition, she washed and hung the clothes. And my mother took me and my older brother John with her sometimes because she had nobody to watch us. I didn't understand none of that at the time, but now I do. And I am so glad that I don't have to live like that. I thank God for His love for all mankind. Now my grandchildren don't have to go through the horrible lifestyle being Desegregated. And I thank all the people that are gone and those that are still alive. For All of the beatings, the abuse, the love, faithfulness, and the biggest of all the strength they showed for us. I thank Kennedy brothers for being the men they were. It took a lot of guts and a big oversized heart to do this. I also thank God for Dr. Martin Luther King which had done a lot of wonderful things.

Mom M (Mom Margaret) and Pop Pop

MOM M

You are so Sweet.
I will never find another Mom as Neat.
You make me Feel my Heartbeat
As my God Mom, to me you are like a Treat.

MOM I LOVE YOU SO DEAR.
Nobody knows the Love
That your Name brings to my Ear.

Mom M. your Love has a Feel
That I know is Real.
With a Love like yours so Real,

When my Body is Sick
A Mention of your Name
Tells me I am NOT ill.

POP POP

Pop Pop even though you are like a be Pop,

You are still my big Pop Pop.

I Love You So Much

Because you give a soft Touch.

And though you are Old

You will Surely get a person Told.

When a person get you Wrong,

Your Words become Strong.

I love you so much Pop Pop

And I don't let the GOOD work Stop.

HAPPY MOTHER'S DAY TO ALL THE MOTHERS!

God gave you your Mother
And He gave me my Mother too!

And I Believe You Think
Or Thought your Mother was
Or is the most Special Person in the World,
No matter what she Say or Do.
Because I know I do!

Even when Mother whipped me Wrongfully,
I Loved her Later.
Now I am Grown,
I Feel the same way.

A Mother has that Love
That make you Feel like NO OTHER CAN.

God gave Father and Mother me!
Even though they didn't know I would be.
But God already had me in View.

So what was Mother to do?
Nothing but look at her Stomach and say,
"OH MY, OH ME LOOK AT YOU!"

The little angel God had put in her Womb,
To Grow like a Balloon.

Now I am Here and I am a Mother too,
That's what God will do.

Happy Mother's Day Mother's!
And to all that are Mothers
TO MANY OF THE OTHERS.

WHEN GOD MADE MOTHER'S,
HE MADE DIAMONDS AND JEWELS

When God Made Mother's,
He Made Diamonds and Jewels.
Because NO ONE can be to us
What a Mother can ever be.

God made it that Way.
And that's the way it should Stay!

Because God made Adam and Eve,
He didn't make Adam and Steve.
Somebody has MESSED UP,
They want to be Adam and Jacob.

But God made Woman to be Mothers,
Not Adam, Jacob, or John!
Or any of the Brothers.
Just us Precious Women that are Mothers.

Happy Mother's Day to all the Mothers.

God gave your Mother to you.
And you to your Mother.
And that's a very special Bond.
Even when it is Wrongfully done.

A Mother has that Love
That make you Feel
Like NO OTHER CAN.

Even sometimes when guys Think
They are to Grown to Cry.
Mother gives them Love
That make them FORGET they are a Man.

GRANDMOTHER

Grandmother I LOVE YOU.

I know I haven't said it in a While,

But I'm saying it Now.

You don't have to Wonder how I said it

AND I REALLY DO.

I LOVE YOU.

I WILL SAY 1 AND 2,

Look up at me, this BIG KISS is for you.

Cause you my Boo.

Grandmother,

I LOVE YOU, AND YOU ARE MY BOO.

Is that OK with you?

Cause if not I will still Love you,

Peek a Boo!

Grandmother,

I remember when I was just a little person

You were there for me,

Thank you.

I remember when you would give me a Dime

And sometimes a Quarter,

I thought I had a lot of Money,

And back then I did.

THANK YOU AGAIN.

CHAPTER 6
My Photos of Me and My Family

Just Chillin'

ABOUT THE AUTHOR

Gwendolyn Victoria Johnson was born on February 4, 1959 to a young mother named Daisy Lee Johnson of Mobile, Alabama. She is a single mother who has raised 3 beautiful boys. She currently a Christian and resides in Delaware.

www.ingramcontent.com/pod-product-compliance
Lightning Source LLC
Chambersburg PA
CBHW070545300426
44113CB00011B/1799